REVIEWERS' COMMENTS ON ALCHEMY, GEMSTONES, THE PLANETS AND YOU

"Wow, an amazing read! Alchemy, gemstones, the planets and sublime literary mastery. This book clearly stimulates you to question your spiritual philosophy. Truly from the invisible to the visible, provocatively addressing the magic and science of alchemy. I recommend Sravaniya and her teachings for anybody on a spiritual quest. A toolbox must have."

— Claire Graham, Psychic & Medium

"We live at such an exciting time on our planet when the teachings of quantum mechanics and our understanding of energy, frequencies and vibration enable us to have a clearer understanding of what the ancient teachings have tried to tell us. We also have the freedom to explore and to think for ourselves.

As we move from the old paradigm of classical physics with its clockwork mechanistic view of the nature of reality, we begin to comprehend what the ancient teachings and traditions knew so well: All is energy and it is vibrating at different frequencies; that everything is connected to everything else and therefore influenced by everything else.

Sravaniya DiPecoraro's excellent book shows us how, as we become aware of these energies and the properties and frequencies of the reality around us, we can harness them to empower us and enhance our lives. Instead of trying to subdue nature or to resist it, we can work in a spirit of cooperation and thus make our lives so much more harmonious.

A truly insightful and informative book."

— Anne Acushla Hassett, Intuitive Coach, Psychic, Hand Analyst, Author

ALCHEMY, GEMSTONES, THE PLANETS AND YOU

TRANSFORMATION AND TRANSCENDENCE

SRAVANIYA DIPECORARO

BAREFOOT · PHILOSOPHER

BP

PRESS

The cover image originally appeared in the Great Lenormand Tarot (J. M. Simon, 1977).

Library of Congress Cataloging-in-Publication Data
DiPecoraro, Sravaniya
Alchemy, Gemstones, the Planets and You
1. New Age 2. Yoga 3. Spirituality and religion

ISBN: 978-988-99111-4-0 (paperback)
ISBN: 978-988-99111-5-7 (ePub)
ISBN: 978-988-99111-6-4 (Kindle)

Barefoot Philosopher Press
P. O. Box 7892
General Post Office
Hong Kong

www.BarefootPhilosopher.Press

To all spiritual seekers, wherever they may be.

CONTENTS

I washed up on the shores of Hong Kong in December 1989 alone and unattended. I had barely survived the sinking of an abusive twelve year marriage with an American Hare Krishna ex-junkie via a Taiwanese divorce — the wife walks and takes nothing with her. My two sons stayed with him and were about to find out why stepmothers historically make such offensive antagonists in literature. I had worked freelance as an English tutor and yoga instructor and, when the NT$ depreciated 25%, I migrated out. Decisions make themselves when the time is right.

Finding my feet in a foreign country was difficult. With no family and almost no friends — I had a few students who knew me from Taiwan — I had to make it with no earthly support. It was in this situation that I delved into astrology and Tarot divination for guidance. Initially I was sceptical but, having no recourse, I gave it a chance. I learned to read cards from a book and the objective information was so accurate that I made time to read for myself daily. Tarot is a relatively quick and easy way of seeing a situation. It is the most objective process of reviewing real options and outcomes that I have ever found.

Then I met Barbara Ellen. I had heard about this visiting psychic from Great Britain in our small new age community in the early 90s so I went for a reading. When she got to work and began telling me of all kinds specifics that she had no ordinary way of knowing, I was astounded. It was then that I was convinced about mediumship and spirit communication. I later found a booklet she had written called *Crystal Energy* (LLangollen Holistic Health Centre, published 1991). I began using it as a guide for wearing gemstones and Barbara Ellen proved reliable once again. Her references and notes on influences of the stones are included in this book.

When it comes to numerical and astrological attribution there are several different systems which are recognized. I studied Cheiro's numerical system, with its roots in Vedic texts, as well as the works of astrologer Lloyd Cope and his mentor Florence Campbell. During application in reading charts these latter two turned out to be the most useful and their system is described herein.

As for astrologers, my greatest influential guides have been Stephen Arroyo, Isabel M. Hickey and Liz Greene. I cannot recommend them highly enough.

My spiritual knowledge comes through my guru His Divine Grace A.C. Bhaktivedanta Swami Prabhupada (founder of ISKCON) of the Brahma-Madhva-Gaudīya-Vaiṣṇava Sampradāya. The section on Spiritual Alchemy (and indeed my entire life) is illuminated by his sublime teachings.

My attitude, for better or worse, has always been that I'm not that interested in what anyone believes. Tell me what you *know*. The truth works when put into practice.

If the doctrine doesn't do what its proponent claims, then it is not real knowledge.

With my spiritual training as an initiate it seems that I live with a foot in each of two worlds. The spiritual side is, of course, most important. But for at least the remainder of this life we all have to continue "chopping wood and carrying water" in time and space. And so I encourage others to develop a deeper, practical understanding of the laws of Nature and Nature's God.

May the facts and insights presented herein bring benefit and assistance to the reader on his or her life's path.

Offered on the 21st of December, 2017
The disappearance day of Śrīla Jīva Gosvāmī
Hong Kong

PART I

THE LECTURE

ALCHEMY, GEMSTONES, THE PLANETS AND YOU
(FULL LECTURE)

by Sravaniya DiPecoraro
Delivered as a lecture in English and Cantonese to a
general audience at the Hong Kong City Hall,
on November 6, 2001.

Thank you all for taking the time to come out this evening and expand your understanding of life and the world in which we live. The purpose of tonight's presentation is to stimulate thought so that you can form your own conclusions. I am presenting some historical facts along with the views of the Bhāgavat Vedānta philosophical school as a point of departure to catalyze this process.

If this presentation moves you to question your assumptions about spirituality and come to some better conclusions, then I will have attained my objective.

This talk is about Planetary Gemnology and I am going to begin by explaining what is alchemy. This is a topic that you can find in the encyclopedia, but what I would like to share with you this evening is some information that you will not find in those pages, because alchemy has an external or exoteric presentation as well as an esoteric or internal meaning.

The word alchemy means to transmute one form of matter into another, or to change material energy. The current New Age movement is really the Old Age in a new bottle. In it you will find identifying characteristics such as a preoccupation with seeing into the future with Tarot cards and other forms of divination, astrology, angels, essential oils and potions for invoking different states of consciousness and mood, crystals and gemstones for healing and controlling energy, etc. This is the outside appearance of the alchemical movement which really goes back to the dawn of the Christian era. It arose in Alexandria, a port city on the coast of North Africa which was a great center of culture and learning, and was Cleopatra's capital in Egypt. This is where many of the texts for all these things we are going to be talking about originated. The alchemical traditions of Alexandria in the first centuries AD developed side by side with Neoplatonic and Hermetic philosophy. And so if you look at the current New Age movement you will see old

Egyptian magical rituals, Gnostic Christianity, and a mixture of various pagan beliefs from Greco-Roman times. Add to the soup some Platonic philosophy and you have the beginning of the movement that we are seeing now.

Astrology was part of that worldview. Astrology speaks of a unity of all things, and a law of what is called signatures or correspondences by which the archetypal realm of God reveals itself through progressively denser material forms. Alchemy went underground during the early medieval period because the Church considered it heretical and, being practiced in secret, its tenets have come to be known as occult (hidden) knowledge.

Being banned in Christian countries, alchemy found sanctuary in Byzantium (later renamed Constantinople, or modern Istanbul). It resurfaced in the west in the 13th century with the Crusaders and especially the Knights Templar. When Constantinople fell in 1453 a lot of writings were recovered, including some teachings of Plato. But since Plato believed in reincarnation, the Church left him aside in favor of Aristotle. St. Thomas Aquinas, whose theology forms the basis of modern Catholic doctrine, based his philosophy on the views of Aristotle.

Interestingly enough, some texts made their way into the collection of one Cosimo de Medici, a wealthy businessman and politician in Florence at the time. Medici handed over these manuscripts to his translator, Marsilio Ficino, to have the Greek rendered into Latin. But when Medici was informed about the magical texts he was so excited that he said "Plato can wait. Translate these first."

The texts were full of alchemical recipes, magical procedures, instructions on the making of talismans, rules for the invocation of planetary deities, and instructions and techniques for seeing into the future by various means.

The Renaissance, which included alchemy, resulted directly from the acquisition of these Neoplatonic and Hermetic texts, many of which came through Alexandria. That is the story regarding the external. The internal metaphysical and psychological development that is alchemy is what is being presented in the doctrines of Jungian depth psychology.

It might be said that when the study of chemistry and the study of the human psyche were separated, that was the beginning of the split between science and religion.

Now one of the newest, and I feel most important, trends in science, healing and thought nowadays is the idea of the interpenetration of dimensions of reality. In this worldview there are subtle and grosser planes of existence and what happens on the subtle or inner plane eventually manifests on the outer plane. If you have attended any of my lectures before you may have heard me describe the four elements as the four levels of human experience. The outer earth plane, the one you can see when I am standing here talking to you, this is the one you can perceive with your five senses. This is the one that modern positivistic science measures.

But science does not know much about these other levels which constitute the inner planes. The level symbolized by water is the emotional level. You can't see it or measure it, but it's real. Indeed, more than any other factor the quality of this level determines the health of the physical body. If there is confusion, fear or distress on the emotional level, that will be experienced eventually on the physical level. Above the emotional level is the level of the mind or thinking. This is more subtle and is correlated with air. Above that is the will, symbolized by fire. Now according to Vedānta, or yoga philosophy, there is something higher than this and that is the ātma or self.

The idea of interpenetration says that these three subtle levels penetrate down into the grosser physical level, and if you know the science you can do something on the physical level to influence the emotional and mental planes also. As our previous speaker this evening was pointing out, progress on the physical or outer plane only is not real progress. A holistic method is to approach the human being on all four levels.

I will be talking about gemstones in just a moment but I'm going to start with a chart. This is a horoscope. I don't know if you've ever seen a horoscope before — and perhaps you cannot see it very well from where you are sitting — but it is a circle with a lot of little squiggles on it that the astrologer can read. How to read a horoscope and what these symbols mean is something that came along with the texts from Alexandria. Astrology is the language of Nature. It speaks of the state of an individual human being on these four levels. It need not be restricted to a human being. Even a chicken or a bridge — it can be the horoscope of any entity. I only do human charts, although I have been requested to do dog charts. I refused... no offense to our canine pals intended.

Now human beings are extremely complex and often contradictory creatures. For example, someone can be very caring and then on the other hand be a real control freak. You may not know anybody like that but I certainly have known a few. The problem then becomes how one can adjust all these things so that the right facet of the personality comes forward in the right situation. What I am getting at is that this birth chart is an Xray of an energy field which contains conscious parts and unconscious parts. The purpose of psychology is to discover and deal with the unconscious complexes which are inconveniently intruding, make them known and integrate them into the conscious personality. Often there is an imbalance.

Now in this particular chart there is trouble with one of the planets (Venus). This client of mine sent me an email today saying that her boyfriend broke up with her. I had only seen her six weeks ago and she wrote something like "I don't seem to recall you saying it was going to be this dreadful."

I can see here what kind of karma or fate is written (Moon conjunct Pluto square to Venus, a singleton in water in the 3rd house) and I wrote back and practically described what had happened — she confirmed that I was right. But what the chart tells me is that she needs more of a particular kind of energy, and one that can be drawn effectively with a gemstone. Before we finish our talk tonight I'll show you how you can find your imbalance, and hopefully prescribe a gemstone just for you — free of charge, of course!

My problem was this: I have studied so many different kinds of systems and presentations of correlation of gemstones with numbers and planets over the years and all of them disagree on certain points. So what I determined to do was put them side by side for comparison and see where they overlap. I took five systems and looked to see if they agreed on any particular points. I'll show you my findings in just a moment.

Back to the four levels. Now these are obviously invisible planes—your emotional level, your mental level, your will power. The outer, physical plane is the only visible part of your life. But you may wonder how is it and by what mechanism do the inner planes interpenetrate into your physical body. I am convinced that it happens through the chakra/endocrine system. There are seven chakras or centers of experience in the human body and each one corresponds to a certain glandular center. Each one is ruled by a different planet and each planet has a different number. So if you know the number and the planet, and you know which gland rules the problem that you have, then you can find out which stone to use. Are you with me? Good.

Let's look at the details. I won't bore you with the agonizing account of my search but I finished it just in time for tonight. I examined the Vedic system, then a system used by Florence Campbell who was a famous numerologist and mystic in the US in the 1930s, Parker's astrology, Alan Oken—all of them are well known in their fields. I have come up with a synthesis.

Let's begin with the Sun. This is what one aspires after,

what one is becoming or embodying in this life. If you were born when the Sun was transiting through the sign of Scorpio you might say, "I'm a Scorpio." But there is more to it than that. The Sun's signature is number 1. This is a luminary in the sky and we all see it every day, but it is also a metal in the earth (gold) and an organ in the body (the heart). It also rules the circulation of the blood, the health of the spinal cord and the physical growth. I had a client who had the Sun in a difficult position in the chart (intercepted in Leo in the 7th House square to Saturn) and she was having trouble with confidence and self esteem. So a person who needs to become more confident, find more sense of her own identity, not relying so much on approval from other people, to have the courage of her convictions, be more bold, courageous and move forward—that person needs a ruby. Or, if you cannot afford a ruby, then there are uparatnas as they are known in Sanskrit, or semi-precious stones that will do the trick.

This is a string of garnets. If you wear a ruby or a garnet what do you get? Of course it depends upon the clarity, the quality, the fire of the stone, the color. But if you get a really good one then it "energizes the body, encourages leadership and gives the confidence needed to make decisions. Wearing this stone enhances your blood circulation, brings more life into the body, it removes sadness and too much sensuality." And gold also purifies and energizes the body, improves circulation, balances the hemispheres of the brain and aids in tissue regeneration. Here in Hong Kong we see pure gold a lot in shops and it is very smart to wear pure gold — although you may not want to wear too much of it in certain parts of town. But anyway it is good for your health and consciousness.

I will go a little more quickly through these now, answer some of your questions and show you how you can find what you need. My client a moment ago who had trouble with her boyfriend had a difficult Venus, so let's take a closer look at this. Venus, which you might say is the planet of love and sharing, corresponds to the number 3, and it has to do with the immune system, the thymus gland and the heart chakra. Venus has to do with personal love, though not necessarily married love. Marriage is very often a deal between two families or nowadays between two consenting adults. Personal love has to do with taste, preference, style that is totally individual. So she should have an emerald because its vibration strengthens the heart, the immune and the nervous system. It also enhances dreams and meditation and is a strong emotional balancer. Guess what else is good for Venus — jade. Jade is also good for your hair and skin, your complexion, the urinary tract and so on. And jade is beneficial to the reproductive system, which must be why it is so popular amongst Chinese women. The Sun, Venus and also Jupiter are considered auspicious vibrations and are often recommended to be invoked.

Let's talk about the Moon next, which corresponds to the number 2. The Moon rules silver and in human anatomy the sympathetic nervous system and the lymphatic system, sometimes described as the dishwater of the body that flushes toxins. It also rules the breasts, uterus and ovaries as well as the unconscious mind. What corresponds to the Moon is pearl, moonstones — the bluish,

waxy looking stones which I have here on my bracelet —
and white zircon.

Mercury is for the general nervous system and this is the
number 7. There is an old system of numerology used in
the 19th century by Count Louis Hamon (1866-1936)
better known as Cheiro, a renowned occultist. Is anyone
familiar with him? He gives the number 5 for Mercury
and interestingly enough the Vedic system does, too. But
after my research I've been applying the newer system
used by Florence Campbell and Lloyd Cope — and it
appears to be working. Mercury has its own stones
(aquamarine and peridot).

Jupiter is 6, Mars is 5 and Saturn is 4 — stable but
rather routine. Mars and Saturn are referred to in the
older astrological texts as malefic. They are difficult or
stressful energies, but everyone has these in their chart.
Saturn corresponds with two numbers, 4 and 8, the latter
of which is shared with Uranus. The number 22 also goes
with Uranus and is the technological number, the vibration for the Age of Aquarius. Then there is Neptune
which is 11, and Pluto which is 9.

These astrological symbols are known as glyphs, which
are highly evocative of much more information than an
English word.

Do you have a little scrap of paper and a pen? I will show you a technique you can use to see what your challenges are. Then we will look up what kind of gemstone you need.

Working out an astrological chart is in depth and gives a tremendous amount of information and detail but it takes longer. It is a tool, but I also like to use numbers because they are much faster and get immediately to the heart of the matter. Now interestingly enough when I worked out my client's numerology the same Venus problem was reflected there.

I'd like for you to write down your birthdate putting the month first, the day second and the year last. Using our example:

August 12, 1972
8 — 12 — 1972
12 minus 8 equals 4.

Subtract either the day from the month or the month from the day, whichever is smaller. This gives you the challenge in the first half of your life. Did anybody get a two digit number? Add the two digits together and get a single number. What did you get? 10 reduces to 1. You need a ruby or a garnet. What else has come up?

Audience: I got a 7.

You need more Mercury and I will explain that in everyday language. This indicates that some weakness or potential problem exists in regard to the lungs or bronchial tubes, the general nervous system—which means you need to take sufficient rest. There may be a problem with the hands or tongue, because Mercury rules all these. So what you need is an aquamarine. Aquamarine sharpens the intellect and the memory, improves learning ability. It improves communication so that you come across to others more clearly. It is said to give clairvoyance and is good for general health and the nervous system. Gives reassurance when you are discouraged and imparts clarity of mind and creative self-expression. Does anyone else have a question?

Audience: What about a person born the 1st of January?

Let's see what the rest of the birthdate yields. Back to my client again, if I subtract her day of birth from the year: 1972 − 12 = 1960. Then I add 1 + 9 + 6 = 16, 1 + 6 = 7. Therefore 7 is the challenge in the second half of life. She also needs Aquamarine during that period.

Now if we take the two sub-challenge numbers and subtract the smaller 4 from the larger 7 we get 3 as the major challenge of the entire life, which is something that a person must always keep in mind and work with.

Audience: I want to ask: The 4 is the first part of life and the 7 is the second part of life. What age is the dividing factor?

I would say about age 35 - 40.

Audience: Then the third number?

This is relevant for the entire life. It is the major challenge.

Audience: What is the big challenge represented by 1?

The deficiency of the number 1 is reflected in the inability to make decisions on one's own, to stand on one's own, being too dependent upon approval from others and a lack of boldness, audacity or courage, and therefore the tendency when confronted with an opportunity to wait, sometimes too long. A ruby or garnet will help enhance your leadership ability. Now all of us are leaders at some time or other, even if it is just our family circle or a couple of friends. Here is a book that I recommend — the best book on numerology on the planet as far as I am concerned, and I've read a few. It talks about the challenges in detail in very straightforward, everyday English. *Your Days Are Numbered* by Florence E. Campbell. I am sure you all will be able to understand it.

Now one more thing. Add them all up and reduce the final total. That is called the life path number and gives an important clue concerning the destiny of the individual. If you get an 11 or 22, don't reduce it for these are master numbers and have their own meaning.

Audience: The earth, water, fire and air elements, do the planets rule those?

No, the signs that the planets are in at the time of birth influence those. We count up the planets in the signs to see the balance. My own method is 2 counts for whatever element the Sun is in, 2 for the Moon, 1 each for the Ascendant and Midheaven, and 1 for each of the other planets, giving special attention to Saturn. This client of mine has nothing in water except Venus, which in astrological parlance is a "singleton" and emphasizes the awkwardness of the Venus challenge number 3.

What follows is my attempt to bring together the best of all the systems which I have studied over the years.

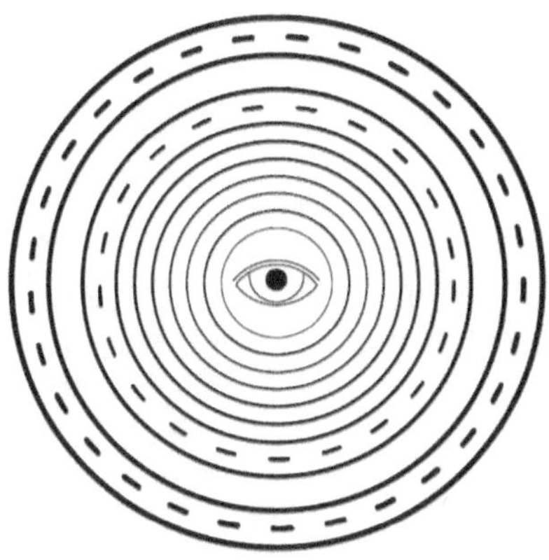

1 Sun — The heart; circulation of the blood, well-being of the spinal cord, physical growth.

Ruby: Energies encourage leadership and give the confidence needed to make decisions. Enhances circulation. Vitalizes blood and the entire system. Removes sadness and sensuality.

Garnet: In addition to the above, it enhances imagination. Strengthens, purifies and vitalizes.

Gold: Purifies and energizes the physical body. Improves circulation and balances the hemispheres of the brain. Aids tissue regeneration and attracts positive energy into the aura.

2 MOON — Ovaries, uterus, breasts, tear ducts, stomach, sympathetic nervous system, lymphatic system.

Moonstone: Strengthens mental faculties. Calms emotions and increases peace of mind. Healing affinity with the stomach, spleen, pancreas and pituitary gland, and helps to unblock the lymphatic system.

Pearl: Good for emotional protection. Can help access unconscious material, release and balance emotional experiences.

Zircon: Strengthens the mind. Aids bowel problems and sleep.

Silver: Enhances mental functions. Aids circulation and strengthens the blood. Improves speech and emotional balance.

7 MERCURY — General nervous system, hands, tongue, thyroid gland, vocal cords, bronchial tubes, lungs, hearing and sight. Respiration, reflexes and nervous functions.

Aquamarine: Improves psychic powers, sharpens intellect, intuition, and memory. Improves learning ability, communication and clairvoyance. Good for general health, especially the nervous system. Gives reassurance when feeling discouraged. Enhances clarity of mind and aids creative self expression.

Peridot: In addition to the above, balances glandular system, aids tissue regeneration and stimulates the mind, accelerates learning. Is also considered a charm against snake bite.

Green Tourmaline: Same as aquamarine and peridot.

Mercury is the metal ruled by the planet Mercury and corresponds with the nervous system and lungs.

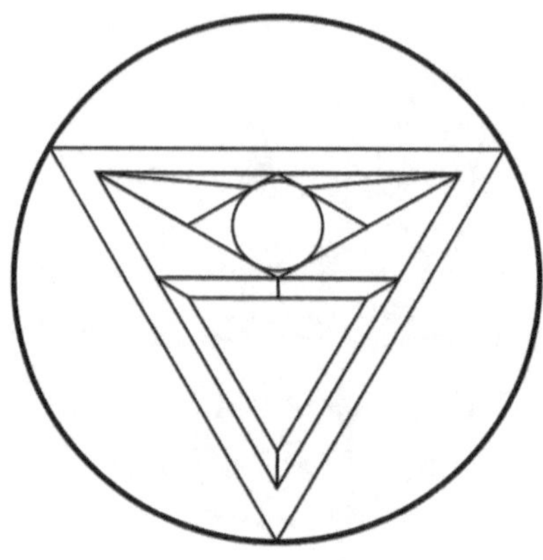

3 VENUS — Hair, skin, complexion and facial features; kidneys, urinary tract, thymus gland, venous circulation of the blood, reproductive system.

Emerald: Strengthens the heart, liver, kidney, immune and nervous systems. Enhances dreams and meditation. Strong emotional balancer.

Jade: Identical with emerald. Cleanses the blood, increases longevity and fertility. Aids eye disorders and female problems.

Copper: Influences the flow of blood and aids in metabolism.

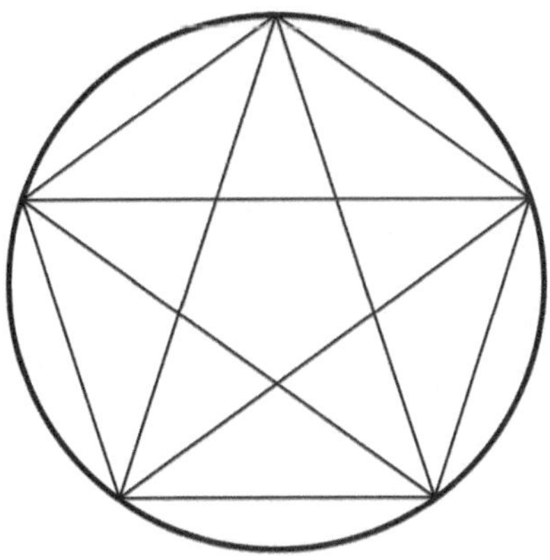

5 MARS — Red corpuscles of the blood, the external reproductive organs and the sex urge; excretory organs, adrenal gland, the muscular tissues and the nose.

Bloodstone: Removes obstacles and averts warfare. Assists in money related matters. Purifies the blood and cures boils. Oxygenates and strengthens the blood and its flow. Helps with iron deficiency and reduces stress.

Chalcedony: Promotes emotional honesty; gently helps one cross over grief, sadness and regret to a state of peace.

Carnelian: Helps increase optimism; aids the kidneys, lungs, liver and gall bladder.

Iron and steel: Enhances blood, muscles and circulation.

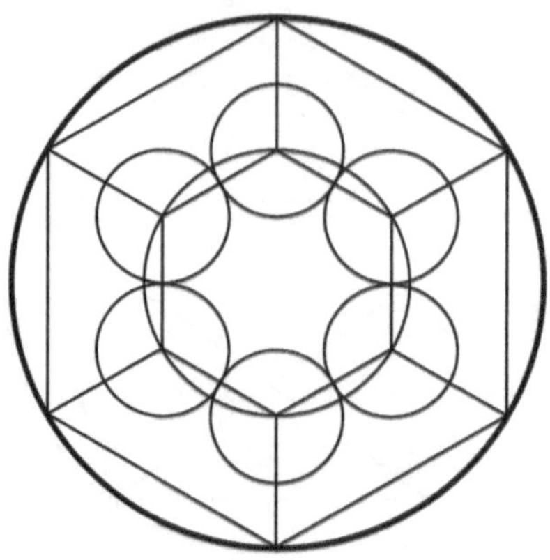

6 JUPITER — Liver, hip joints, thighs, intestines, blood plasma, and the posterior pituitary gland. Concerned with cell nutrition and development, as well as the formation of hemoglobin.

Topaz: Promotes general well being and spiritual knowledge. Especially helpful in pregnancy, childbirth and marriage. Prevents jaundice and liver diseases. Increases generosity, happiness, humor, optimism and hope. Aids tissue regeneration and detoxifies the body.

Amethyst: Heightens spiritual awareness and intuition. Enhances psychic ability and evolution. Protects from hidden enemies and mysterious dangers and diseases, from drowning, intoxication, addiction and government punishment. Brings fortune to gamblers.

Yellow Sapphire: Same as topaz.

Citrine: Same as topaz. Brings mental clarity and spiritual intelligence (separating the relevant from the irrelevant), strengthens intuitive perceptions. Enhances physical healing energy and diminishes self-destructive tendencies. Raises self-esteem. Good for kidneys, colon, liver, heart and tissue regeneration. Attracts abundance.

Amber: Exerts a positive influence on the endocrine system, spleen and heart. Soothes and harmonizes.

Tin: Positively affects the liver and gall bladder.

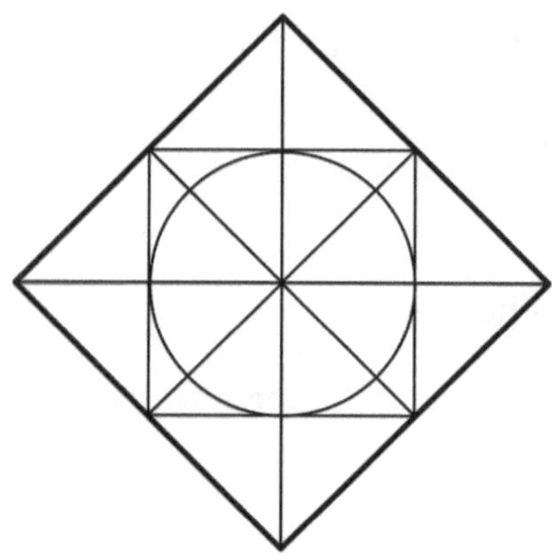

4 / 8 SATURN — Skin, bones, joints, teeth, ligaments, knees, calf, spleen and the organs of hearing. Ossification, congestion, the proper functioning of the tendons and cartilage.

Blue Sapphire: Strengthens the heart and kidneys. Stimulates psychic abilities, clarity and inspiration. Counteracts enviousness from others and keeps away the evil eye. Protects from travel dangers and mental unrest. Alleviates long-term misfortune.

Lapis Lazuli: Same as sapphire. Releases tension and anxiety.

Lead: Good for the bones, skin, hair and nails.

8 / 22 URANUS — The part of the eye that can see the human energy field. The electricity that passes between the nerve cells. Higher intuition.

Hessonite: Helps avert disaster, insanity, poison, and evil spirits. Gives genius in sciences. Improves dealings with confused and helpless people and protects from sudden misfortunes.

Yellow-orange Zircon: Same as above.

11 NEPTUNE — Pineal gland; those parts of the nervous system that are receptive to psychic impression. The functioning of the chakras and the human aura.

Amethyst: Improves psychic movements. Protects from hidden enemies and mysterious dangers and diseases. Protects from drowning, intoxication, addiction and government punishment. Brings fortune to gamblers.

Cat's Eye: Same as amethyst. Enhances will-power and helps one act wisely (feet firmly planted on the ground). Benefits the spleen, pancreas, digestive organs and colon. Helps soften stubbornness. Enhances perception and insight.

Platinum: Positive influences for psychic receptivity.

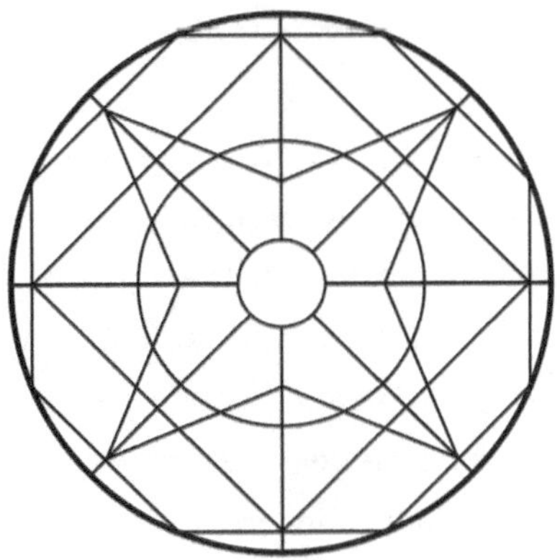

9 PLUTO — Creative and regenerative processes. In particular, Pluto rules conception, the well being of the reproductive organs, and the anabolic and catabolic phases of metabolism.

Coral: Removes obstacles and averts warfare. Assists in money related matters. Purifies the blood and cures boils.

Opal: Aids eyesight and balances emotion. Enhances intuition. Its full spectrum of color resonates with all the chakras.

Black Obsidian: Symbolizes mastery over the physical plane. Should be treated with respect due to its power, but is ideal for over-emotional states as it stabilizes compulsive and erratic energies.

DIAMOND AND TURQUOISE

What about Diamond? It induces purity, honesty and fearlessness (Sun). Gives artistic abilities (Venus) and worldly happiness (Jupiter). Strengthens bones (Saturn) and is useful for diseases of the sex organs (Mars). That about covers all the bases. With its affinity with 6 it stands for harmony, a necessity for married life. Barbara Ellen says it "purifies the etheric bodies and dispels negativity."

Turquoise: A healing stone. Alleviates over-acidity, pain, rheumatism, gout, stomach problems, cramps and viral infections. Increases muscular strength. Detoxifying.

Attracts power, friendships, luck and happiness. Releases shame and guilt. "Turkish stone" protects horse riders from injuries due to falls.

Conclusion

I will leave you with a story. The Greek myth of Prometheus tells us a curious thing about jewelry. There was once a titan or giant named Prometheus who saw the plight of mankind and took pity upon them. There they were, struggling to get along and Prometheus thought to himself, "How much better it would be if they had some fire. But fire is only for the gods… Still, I bet I could steal some and give it to the people." With the best of intentions, Prometheus went up to heaven, took some fire and concealed it in the hollow of a fennel stalk and brought it down to earth. For this intelligent, expedient and supremely charitable act toward a race not his own, Prometheus was arrested by the king of the gods, Zeus, and imprisoned—chained to a rock in the Caucasus mountains. There he suffered greatly all alone.

Meanwhile Zeus was determined to undo some of the good that the Titan had done. He ordered Vulcan the smith god to create a woman of dazzling beauty, perfect of form and limb, but without intelligence and with lies in her mouth. Then Zeus had the smith fashion a box into which he put all the curses of man — old age, insanity, incontinence, fear, the works. These he sent to Prometheus' brother Epimetheus who, after seeing what his brother got for defying the king of the gods, accepted her gratefully without complaint. Although she was forbidden to open the box, Pandora did so anyway and now all of us get the flu, wrinkles and gray hair.

But the reason why I am telling you this story is this: After a long and agonizing time, Prometheus made an arrangement and was finally released from his confinement. But Zeus took a piece of the rock to which he had been chained and a bit of the iron chain itself and had a ring fashioned for Prometheus to wear, so that he would remember never to defy the gods again. A memento, a reminder, a fiat against rebellion and anarchy.

What we wear has such powerful effect upon our consciousness and our behavior, and yet it is something within our free will to choose. Let's choose wisely.

PART II

FOR THOSE WHO WANT TO KNOW MORE

Real Knowledge

This section is based on pramāṇa - knowledge supported with evidence. The definition is given in the Yoga Sutras of Patañjali.

प्रत्यक्षानुमानागमाः प्रमाणानि
pratyakṣa-anumāna-āgamāḥ pramāṇāni
"Correct knowledge is direct, inferred or proven as factual."
— Yoga Sutras I.7

1. pratyakṣa means direct perception (sensual observation).
2. anumāna means logical inference.
3. āgamāḥ means that knowledge acquired from bonafide sacred texts or a person whose authority is in a sacred lineage and does not deviate from these texts.

Of these three sources of information, the first two can be faulty. The senses are not perfect and mistakes are often made. The premise upon which the logical reasoning is based may be incorrect or flawed. However, as we will be discussing in this section, scriptural knowledge handed down in an authorized lineage is infallible — because the source of this knowledge is perfect and infallible. This can be verified by putting the information that can be tested into practice. It works every time it's tried.

Among the sacred texts quoted herein, a few will be abbreviated for faster reference:

Bhagavad-Gītā As It Is — BG
Śrīmad-Bhāgavatam — SB
Caitanya-caritāmṛta — CC
Yoga Sutras of Patañjali — YS

The Laws of Nature

The word alchemy means to transmute one form of matter into another, or to change the form of material energy. In other words, magic. However, this activity is not based upon imagination or belief but rather upon science. For a society that grew up with Harry Potter and entertainment films full of special effects, this idea may take a few minutes to process.

To transmute matter one must understand the laws of Nature and their limitations. And then one must learn how to work within them.

Here are some direct observations (pratyakṣa) from one of my most reliable sources, world renowned astrologer Isabel M. Hickey, in her classic text *Astrology, A Cosmic Science*.

"Nature has an ebb and flow like the tides in the ocean. The tides can be used or neglected. Everything in nature is on the upswing between the New and Full Moon; when its energy starts to recede and is ebbing, the tide is at its greatest passivity before the New Moon. Note the lack of pep and vitality in people in the last phases of the dying Moon. Everything is dragging and only those interested in Cosmic laws know why it is so."

I can attest to the veracity of this statement. When I taught hatha yoga professionally I framed the focus of postures (āsana) in my classes according to the lunar phases. The week of the waning to New Moon I taught restorative poses. Indeed, the students would come and lie down exhausted on their mats before class, like ship-wrecked travelers washed up on the shore.

But beyond this basic example, an individual has a sort of toolbox of personality traits and natural dispositions, manifested from karmic impressions within the subtle body which we generally refer to as mind. These thoughts, emotions and attitudes will be triggered at specific times by planetary movements (transits) and experienced inwardly as happiness, distress; outwardly there will manifest opportunity, relationships, beginnings and endings. The alchemist or magician knows these in advance and, in cooperation with Nature, guides the changes as far as possible.

More from Isabel M. Hickey:

"Knowledge of the tides and currents can be gained a long time before they are flowing so the individual can build in (of his own volition) the necessary ingredients mentally, emotionally and physically. When the time for testing comes he can pass it for he has done the necessary work ahead of time. He uses his energies. They do not use him. This is the proper use of astrology."

Practically speaking, we may consider that astrology is the language of Nature. The horoscope of an individual is a psychological blueprint; a statement of purpose in time and space.

The Language of Nature

Although we cannot, in our present discussion, explain everything there is to know about astrological language, here are a few basic concepts.

THE SIGNS OF THE ZODIAC number twelve. These are actually six pairs of opposites, of dynamic duos, if you will (6 x 2 = 12). They also represent specific qualities of human experience on four levels of reality in three different modes (4 x 3 = 12).

THE ELEMENTS — Levels of Reality:
Air — thought — Libra, Aquarius, Gemini
Fire — will — Aries, Leo, Sagittarius
Water — emotion — Cancer, Scorpio, Pisces
Earth — physical — Capricorn, Taurus, Virgo

THE MODES — Matter has three phases or modes:
moving (cardinal)
inert or steady (fixed)
adjusting (mutable) slowing down or speeding up
depending upon circumstances

THE PLANETS — These are the energy regulators.
They also represent dimensions of human experience.
Sun — identity, the individual
Moon — feeling, reaction

Mercury — communication, mental connection (no moral sense)
Venus — expression, giving, affection, sharing, beauty, waiting (feminine)
Mars — taking, focused effort, assertion, action (masculine)
Jupiter — expansion, inspiration, morality, generosity
Saturn — contraction, constraint, limitation, penurious-ness, conservative
Uranus — ingenuity, innovation, independence, rebellion
Neptune — self-sacrifice, service, martyrdom
Pluto — transformation, intensity, power

THE ASPECTS — These indicate how well the various dimensions of experience are integrated in an individual; they show the "karmic bank account."
Conjunctions — strong inclinations; can be good or not depending on the planets involved.
Trines — karmic credits, natural talent or good fortune that comes on its own due to past piety.
Sextiles — fortunate tendencies, but must be acted upon to yield results.
Oppositions — dualities that must be adjusted, often worked out in relation to others.
Squares — karmic debts (impiety) that will hit one over the head again and again. With knowledge and self control these lessons can actually be turned into char-acter assets, such that the person would be able to train someone else how to overcome the problems.

The birth chart speaks of the state of an individual human being in the present life on these four levels. But how is this possible? And how can astrology specifically predict such things as timing of incidents, relationships and personal characteristics?

We now enter into the rather uncomfortable region of considering destiny or fate — and how we do not have quite as much freedom of choice as we would like to believe. The universal paradox is that we are free to choose but we are not free from the consequences of those choices.

I hereby offer some real life experience (pratyakṣa) for my reader's consideration.

An astrologer's diary
Sunday, August 13, 2017

"Sorcerers say that we are inside a bubble. It is a bubble into which we are placed at the moment of our birth. At first, the bubble is open, but then it begins to close until it has sealed us in. That bubble is our perception. We live inside that bubble all our lives. And what we witness on its round walls is our own reflection."

— Carlos Castaneda, Tales of Power

My mind was very disturbed by my perception of an interaction with another person. The feeling was one of being neglected, unappreciated; that some offense was taken because of a joke I had made. It was a seemingly minor incident but it caused strong feelings within.

What compounded this situation was that I had done a relationship reading for a client regarding her issues with a close associate. That scenario rather reflected identical ones which I could see in my own.

In the middle of the night I could not sleep. So I thought to go and check my transits — i.e. the current movements of the planets triggering my horoscope. What I found was stunning.

A little background first. The horoscope of an individual is like a statement of purpose in time and space. One's karmic impressions for the current life (prārabdha karma) generated by personal actions in the past are imprinted in the psyche or subtle body (manas) at the moment of birth. Planetary movements trigger these complexes which manifest as attitudes, tendencies, feelings, relationships and even physical incidents.

The transits of the Moon to those planetary placements of mine told the entire story of my inner emotional environment. The descriptions I was reading were so specific that I realized my subjective reality was being generated by cosmic movements. That means not only was it a kind of "virtual emotional experience" — not really caused by or even related to anyone else — but it happened right on time.

In other words I, the spirit, was witnessing a storm inside

my mind. It was not actual (Moon opposition Neptune, the emblem of imagination) but only perceived by me individually and quite temporarily, since the effect of Moon transits is brief and lasts at most half a day. And I am not talking about one transit alone — there were four different influences and I was experiencing all of them at once! The complete descriptions were there before me, written in English.

Now I had a choice: to act out based on my inner perceptions and perhaps permanently alter an important relationship, OR to let the storm pass and do nothing — as was suggested by the astrologer writing about one of the transits. Fortunately, due to my regular yoga meditations (sādhana) I had the good sense to go for the second option.

The happiness and distress each one of us experiences at any given moment is not only predestined; moreover it is scheduled. It is delivered right on time. This realization blew me away. Or more accurately it blew away the impulses to avenge myself of the wrong that I perceived had been done to me.

My paean to Material Nature:

How powerful is Fate! How she acts through the mind,
How everything is predestined and delivered right on time.

Everything, that is, except one's response.

Spirit, Mind and Body

These three words are mentioned together and I find it quite telling (of the person speaking) which one comes first. "Body, mind and spirit" seems to give prominence to the body with the other two as appendages; "Mind, body and spirit" gives more psychological importance, with spirit as a kind of nondescript after thought.

Often times when I would do an astrological reading for a client I would come to a point when I had to ask: "Do you consider that you are a body that has a mind and a spirit? Or are you a spirit inhabiting a mind and body?" These two different perspectives are the "fork in the road," if you will; each view gives a different impetus for action with correspondingly different results. Invariably the person with me would identify as a spirit. Somehow this is common sense when put on the table in plain language.

The sacred scripture Bhagavad-Gītā (2.20) covers the relationship between these three in detail. It describes the conscious spiritual living being as "unborn, eternal, ever-existing, undying and primeval." The mind and body are described as subtle and gross matter, which are always changing and are temporary in nature. Spirit is superior energy; material body/mind is inferior energy.

To use the analogy of a computer, body is the hardware,

mind is the software — and spirit is the user. The mind (psyche) or subtle body is used by the will of the conscious living spirit to access the physical body in order to pursue the user's desires. The results of such activities, however, also impress the mind in various ways (vāsanā). Every action has a reaction. These impressions go with the spirit in his subtle covering from one gross body to the next — indeed, they are part of the mechanism that determines what kind of body and life experiences he will get next.

Reality v. Illusion

In this regard I find it important to point out a few major differences in the modern and ancient paradigms of observing reality.

In the modern framework of seeing the world we are told that a person comes into this life with a "blank slate" and is gradually conditioned by his or her environment, childhood and the circumstances encountered therein. The family background and culture are considered responsible for a person's attitudes and even success or failure in life. (Of course, this viewpoint does not explain why someone can come from obscurity or poverty and make something extraordinary of him or herself through hard work, determination and meaningful contribution to society.) This view is the standard basis for claimed victimhood and is often used by unscrupulous men to make a good living off of others' misfortunes, as well as to control social groups to support certain parties or take up certain causes. In that way this viewpoint is useful and effective, whether or not it is true. What is present on the physical plane is taken as what matters most. One's mental perspective creates one's experience and can therefore be altered to make one more accepting — by cajoling, convincing, social pressure, anti-depressant drugs and so on. There is no such thing as good or bad; the main consideration is whether you like it or not.

Moral equivalence has obliterated any discussion of right or wrong; right or left is the new view, which makes one's behavior sound like a mere stylistic preference.

But according to the Vedic paradigm, one gets the situation (parents, social position) he or she deserves, based on his own individual activities in previous lives. The law of karma is really "pay as you go." One's desires and actions produce impressions on the subtle body and it is these that determine what will eventually manifest. Cāṇakya Paṇḍita (ca. 300 BC) stated it thus:

"These five: the life span, the type of work, wealth, learning and the time of one's death are determined while one is in the womb."

— Cāṇakya Nīti-śāstra 4.1

Human beings that obey the laws of Nature and Nature's God are called pious or good, and such actions elevate one's present and future position; those actions that defy Nature's law are impious or sinful and degrade one's position. The direction here is not right or left but rather up or down.

The reality is that what is present on the subtle plane will manifest on the physical plane. Understanding this point will help the reader grasp the concepts herein under consideration.

Signatures and Correspondences

"What is Venus but the artemesia that grows in your garden? And what is iron but the planet Mars? Venus and the artemesia are both of the same essence, while Mars and iron are manifestations of the same cause."

— Paracelsus

The alchemical paradigm postulates a unity of all things, and a law of signatures or correspondences by which the archetypal or "ideal" realm of God or the gods revealed itself through progressively denser material forms.

In the first section of this book the connection has been made between the planets as energy regulators of urges and needs, of planetary rulerships of the physical body. Physical illness is an outer plane manifestation of an inner plane (mental/emotional) issue. Yet the question arises: from where does the issue originate?

The answer is one's own choices and actions. There's that pesky notion of personal responsibility again.

Karma means action or work. Newton's Third Law of physics states, "For every action there is an equal and opposite reaction." This is every bit as true karmically as physically. In line with this reasoning, The Golden Rule says:

"Do unto others as you would have them do unto you."

I would add "… because one day they will."

Karma ~ What You Need to Know

"The exact word used in this connection, yadṛcchayā, means that every living entity has a predestined happiness and distress in his present body; this is called the law of karma."

— Śrīmad-Bhāgavatam, 3.27.8 purport

Nearly all the people I have encountered in New Age circles (many of whom are Catholic and Methodist by the way) consider that the law of karma may, in fact, be real. However, they do not understand it in detail; they seem apprehensive about what they might discover if they did. Personal responsibility is the elephant in the room that people try like anything to ignore, for as long as they do they can get away with blaming everyone else for their misfortunes.

Karma is a profound subject and could take many pages, but my aim is to make it concise and easy to understand. An alternative title for what follows might be Karma for Dummies — except that dummies aren't interested in this subject. Let's get started.

According to Vedic knowledge there are three kinds of karma:

- Present Karma (prārabdha): activities and thoughts carried over from previous lives;

destiny in progress which cannot be prevented; the present body as depicted in the horoscope, which is really a map of an individual process.

- Savings (sancita): the total accumulated stock of karmic deposits (āśaya) from innumerable lifetimes, awaiting fruition.
- Earnings (vartamāna): acquired during the present lifetime and will bear fruit in the future lifetimes. Those subconscious impressions remain in the subtle body and take the spirit to future destinations after the present body is no longer usable.

The Good, the Bad, the Ugly

In his translation of Śrī Īśopaniṣad, Śrīla Prabhupāda makes these observations (Mantra 2 purport):

"Karma, akarma and vikarma are very clearly described in the Bhagavad-Gītā. Actions that are performed in terms of one's prescribed duties, as mentioned in the revealed scriptures, are called karma. Actions that free one from the cycle of birth and death are called akarma. And actions that are performed through the misuse of one's freedom and that direct one to the lower life forms are called vikarma. Of these three types of action, that which frees one from the bondage to karma is preferred by intelligent men. Ordinary men wish to perform good work in order to be recognized and achieve some higher status of life in this world or in heaven, but more advanced men want to be free altogether from the actions and reactions of work. Intelligent men well know that both good and bad work equally bind one to the material miseries. Consequently they seek that work which will free them from the reactions of both good and bad work."

Then there is ugra-karma — distressful activities.

"The materialists, who have no concept of God, think that they are advancing. But, according to Bhagavad-

Gītā, they are unintelligent and devoid of all sense. They try to enjoy this material world to the utmost limit and therefore always engage in inventing something for sense gratification. Such materialistic inventions are considered to be advancement of human civilization, but the result is that people grow more and more violent and more and more cruel, cruel to animals and cruel to other human beings. They have no idea how to behave toward one another. Animal killing is very prominent amongst demoniac people. Such people are considered the enemies of the world because ultimately they will invent or create something which will bring destruction to all. Indirectly, this verse anticipates the invention of nuclear weapons, of which the whole world is today very proud. At any moment war may take place, and these atomic weapons may create havoc. Such things are created solely for the destruction of the world, and this is indicated here. Due to godlessness, such weapons are invented in human society; they are not meant for the peace and prosperity of the world."

— Bhagavad-Gītā, 16.9 purport by Śrīla Prabhupāda

Those who ignore the laws of Nature, who identify themselves as the body and mind are referred to herein as demoniac. Their path leads away from God toward unrestricted sense gratification. And they are encouraged in their quest by those who would benefit financially from their self created misfortune with exhortations like "No limits — no regrets." Actually the truth is exactly the opposite. Human life begins with acceptance of personal responsibility and duty. In a Godless civilization this education is glaringly absent.

"Good people don't need laws to tell them to act respon-
sibly… Bad people will find a way around the laws."
— Plato

If the universe (to "turn as one") were a machine, the Vedas would be the instruction booklet on how to use it — both the benefits and the dangers to avoid (pravṛtti and nivṛtti).

"The Vedas are not compilations of human knowledge. Vedic knowledge comes from the spiritual world, from Lord Kṛṣṇa. Another name for the Vedas is śruti. Śruti refers to that knowledge which is acquired by hearing."

According to authorities of these sacred texts, this knowledge is beyond the four deficiencies of human beings:

- imperfect senses
- tendency to make mistakes
- tendency to cheat
- tendency to fall into illusion (misconceptions)*

*What kind of misconceptions? Ideas such as:

- Everything in life happens by chance or randomly without design.
- Life is a mystery. Nobody knows why things happen.
- I am in control — at least of some things.
- I am this body.

- Matter works by itself. No one is in charge. I can therefore do whatever I want and, if I believe hard enough, I will succeed.
- I can change the world with kindness.
- It's better not to know.

In a society of cheaters and cheated there are many more such memes. Ignorance is always a choice — although lately it seems to have evolved into a fine art.

Vedic Overview

One Veda was divided into four — Rig, Sama, Yajur and Atharva. The summary is called Vedānta-sūtra. There are 108 Upaniṣads and 18 Purāṇas.

Mahābhārata is Vedic knowledge via historical narration, easily digested by everyday people. The Gītā is found here.

Bhagavad-Gītā is also known as Gītopaniṣad. It is the essence of Vedic knowledge and one of the most important Upaniṣads in Vedic literature.

Śrīla Prabhupāda said in a lecture in Los Angeles November 27 in 1968: "Upaniṣads are the headlines of the Vedas. Just like in a chapter, there is a headline, similarly these Upaniṣads are the headlines of the Vedas. There are 108 Upaniṣads, principal. Out of that, nine Upaniṣads are very important."

They are: Śvetāśvatara Upaniṣad, Taittireya Upaniṣad,

Aitareya Upaniṣad, Īśopaniṣad, Īśa Upaniṣad, Muṇḍaka Upaniṣad, Māṇḍūkya Upaniṣad, Kaṭhopaniṣad.

He says further: "And whenever there is argument on some point, one has to give reference from these Upaniṣads." This is known as śabda-pramāṇa. Pramāṇa means evidence.

"In India if one person tells another, "You must do this," the other party may say, "What do you mean? Is this a Vedic injunction, that I have to follow you without any argument?" Vedic injunctions cannot be interpreted. But ultimately, if you carefully study why these injunctions are there, you will find that they are all correct."

— Śrīla Prabhupāda, introduction to Śrī Īśopaniṣad

The Atharva Veda section contains hymns and incantations, often to be recited by a brahmin or sorcerer, which were used as charms and spells to invoke some benefit — cure of a disease, long life for a relative, or even finding a wife or lover. However, the standard of brahminical expertise has diminished so much over the past fifty centuries. Whereas formerly a learned priest could ignite a fire by chanting a mantra pronounced correctly, currently this is no longer possible.

Interestingly enough, in contemporary discussions of these Vedic hymns the relevance of karmic impressions (that is the debts and credits produced by one's past activities in previous lives) is minimized or else entirely absent. There is more focus on curing jaundice, fever or injuries than there is on the fact that material existence is an ongoing flow of the results of of one's own individual activities in the past.

It stands to reason that if there are laws then there must be a lawmaker. If there is a spider web there must be a spider. Spider webs do not simply appear automatically. Neither does this intricate cosmos.

The Lawmaker ~ Īśvara

अहं सर्वस्य प्रभवो मत्तः सर्वं प्रवर्तते।
इति मत्वा भजन्ते मां बुधा भावसमन्विताः ॥१०-८॥
aham sarvasya prabhavo
mattaḥ sarvam pravartate
iti matvā bhajante mām
budhā bhāva-samanvitāḥ

"I am the source of all spiritual and material worlds.
Everything emanates from Me. The wise who know this
perfectly engage in My devotional service and worship
Me with all their hearts."
— Lord Śrī Krishna, BG 10.8

Bhagavad-Gītā (literally the "Song of God") is the
gateway to the ocean of Vedic knowledge. This sacred
scripture is so essential that it forms the basis of six
different philosophical systems in India. It is renowned
throughout the world both east and west. According to
self realized authorities in spiritual science, the speaker is
none other than the Supreme Personality of Godhead
Himself, Lord Śrī Krishna. Accepting this as our
premise, let's hear what He has to say in relation to our
present discussion of gross and subtle energies.

"I shall now declare unto you in full this knowledge, both
phenomenal and numinous [gross and subtle]. This being
known, nothing further shall remain for you to know.

Out of many thousands among men, one may endeavor for perfection, and of those who have achieved perfection, hardly one knows Me in truth.

Earth, water, fire, air, ether, mind, intelligence and false ego – all together these eight constitute My separated material energies.

Besides these, O mighty-armed Arjuna, there is another, superior energy of Mine, which comprises the living entities who are exploiting the resources of this material, inferior nature.

All created beings have their source in these two natures. Of all that is material and all that is spiritual in this world, know for certain that I am both the origin and the dissolution.

O conqueror of wealth, there is no truth superior to Me. Everything rests upon Me, as pearls are strung on a thread."

— Bhagavad-Gītā 7.2-7

For the benefit of human society the Lord compiles Vedic knowledge (BG 15.15). In other words the manufacturer gives the instruction booklet for the universe. Bhagavad-Gītā is the summary of that knowledge for every man and woman.

However, in chapter eight Lord Krishna describes this world as duḥkhālayam aśāśvatam — miserable and temporary.

"From the highest planet in the material world down to the lowest, all are places of misery wherein repeated birth and death take place. But one who attains to My abode, O son of Kunti, never takes birth again."

— Bhagavad-Gītā 8.16

Prabhupāda: "This material world is certified by Śrī Kṛṣṇa, the creator, as *duḥkhālayam* — full of miseries. How then can we make it comfortable? Is it possible to make this world comfortable by the so-called advancement of science? No, this is not possible. As a result, we do not even wish to know what these miseries are. The miseries, as stated before, are birth, old age, disease, and death, and because we cannot make a solution to them, we try to set them aside. Science has no power to solve these miseries that are always giving us trouble. Instead, they divert our attention to the making of spaceships or atomic bombs. The solution to these problems is given here in Bhagavad-gītā: if one attains to Kṛṣṇa's platform he does not have to return again to this earth of birth and death."

— Beyond Birth and Death, Chapter 3

Krishna explains that, as eternal spiritual beings, our real home is in the eternal spiritual realm. He presents the process of yoga as the best means for returning there. Throughout countless lifetimes He continues to reach out to each of us through religious teachings, offering the chance to reconnect with Him in a perfect relationship of eternal love. However, a living being has something called consent. And if one's desire is not to surrender to the Supreme but to stay here in the material world awhile longer, then there are certain rules and guidelines to help him avoid unnecessary trouble.

Laws and rules are meant to keep us safe. We have often heard the saying that "Rules are made to be broken." Consider the fact that the highest paid occupations in the culture where this saying is prominent are lawyers and doctors — persons who rake in the money to be made from others' personal crisis management.

Which brings me to what I consider a salient point that I would now like to address.

True Healing

In 2017 I was giving some Tarot consultations to a few people at a holistic center event. One by one they came into the room for a private session. "I want to be a healer" was the idea that I heard expressed again and again. Indeed, the healing profession seems to be booming with a plethora of techniques from yoga meditation to sound healing baths to essential oil burning, energy healing and on and on.

The question arises: What is the disease?

If the diagnosis is wrong then the wrong remedy will be applied.

During a lecture (Śrīmad-Bhāgavatam 5.5.2) he gave in Durban on October 22, 1975, my guru Śrīla Prabhupāda put it this way.

"We have got two kinds of bodies -- subtle body and gross body. This gross body is made of five gross material elements: earth, water, fire, air, ether... At the time of death this gross body is finished, but the subtle body — mind, intelligence and ego — will carry me to another gross body. ... So the spirit soul is in this way bound up by the material gross body and subtle body. This is our disease. Material existence means we are suffering from this disease."

Gemstones and mantras are helpful in alleviating or creating certain conditions for a limited time. However, the truth is that there is no permanent material solution to any of the problems of life within the material world. The solution, the cure, is spiritual realization. I am not my body or my mind; I am spirit. Forgetfulness of my true nature is the disease.

The reality is that material domination is a false dream. Indeed, a dream is an illusion that never happened. Although tampering with material energy is highly seductive, it is futile to attempt to make arrangements to exist in an atmosphere of non-existence. Whatever one obtains will be lost in the course of time. Bud, bloom and fade are the ways of this world, where the problems of disease, old age, death and (whether you believe in it or not) repeated birth are ongoing. Disappointment and the relentless struggle for existence lead inevitably to anxiety, trauma and depression, which can end up in addiction and death.

Or it can spur one to search for the Absolute Truth.

Here is an excerpt from Bhagavad-Gītā 2.7 purport.

"Who is the man in material perplexities? It is he who does not understand the problems of life. In the Garga Upanishad the perplexed man is described as follows:

yo va etad akṣaraṁ gārgi aviditvāsmāl lokāt praiti sa kṛpaṇaḥ

"He is a miserly man who does not solve the problems of life as a human and who thus quits this world like the cats and dogs, without understanding the science of self-realization."

Now we come to the ultimate in human potential, the greatest work an individual can undertake — the Magnum Opus.

Spiritual Alchemy

"This process is the supreme intelligence of the intelligent, the cleverness of the most clever, for by following it one can in this very life make use of the temporary and unreal to achieve Me, the eternal reality."

— Lord Śrī Krishna to Uddhava, SB 11.29.22

The real purpose of human life is spiritual self-realization, beyond the temporary sensual gratification of eating, sleeping, mating and defending of animal existence. What am I? I am spirit (brahman). Self-realization means to understand that my nature is eternal, full of knowledge and happiness.

But there is more: What is my purpose? To serve the Great Spirit, the Supreme Cause of all Causes, in an eternal loving relationship. This is God-realization. Each of us has an eternal, personal relationship with Him. Unfortunately we have temporarily forgotten it.

It should be noted that self means person and that Higher Self means Supreme Person. Without two persons there is no possibility of loving exchange. When the self wants to understand the Higher Self, that is yoga.

In the old days I often heard the word yoga in conjunction with various prefixes indicating a lineage or school. More recently I have noticed that some instructors are now even adding their own names as a prefix. This is what branding and marketing looks like. But in the Bhagavad-Gītā there are only three types of yoga discussed — karma yoga, jñāna yoga and bhakti yoga. Actually these are levels of realization, not "styles" or options at a yoga buffet.

Krishna, the master of yoga (Yogeśvara), gives His opinion thus:

योगिनामपि सर्वेषां मद्गतेनान्तरात्मना।
श्रद्धावान्भजते यो मां स मे युक्ततमो मतः ॥ ६-४७॥
yoginām api sarveṣāṁ
mad-gatenāntar-ātmanā
śraddhāvān bhajate yo māṁ
sa me yukta-tamo mataḥ

"And of all yogis, he who always abides in Me with great faith, worshiping Me in transcendental loving service, is most intimately united with Me in yoga and is the highest of all." (BG 6.47)

In the purport Prabhupāda gives a detailed explanation which is worth reading:

"*Yoga* actually means *bhakti-yoga*; all other *yogas* are progressions toward the destination of *bhakti-yoga*. From the beginning of *karma-yoga* to the end of *bhakti-yoga* is a long way to self-realization. *Karma-yoga*, without fruitive results, is the beginning of this path. When *karma-yoga* increases in knowledge and renunciation, the stage is called *jñāna-yoga*. When *jñāna-yoga* increases in meditation on the Supersoul by different physical processes, and the mind is on Him, it is called *aṣṭāṅga-yoga*. And, when one surpasses the *aṣṭāṅga-yoga* and comes to the point of the Supreme Personality of Godhead Kṛṣṇa, it is called *bhakti-yoga,* the culmination. Factually, *bhakti-yoga* is the ultimate goal, but to analyze *bhakti-yoga* minutely one has to understand these other *yogas.* The *yogi* who is progressive is therefore on the true path of eternal good fortune. One who sticks to a particular point and does not make further progress is called by that particular name: *karma-yogi, jñāna-yogi* or *dhyāna-yogi, rāja-yogi, haṭha-yogi, atha-yogi,* etc. If one is fortunate enough to come to the point of *bhakti-yoga,* it is to be understood that he has surpassed all the other *yogas.*"

Although bhakti is the topmost yoga, the seeker doesn't necessarily have to move step by step through each of the stages before achieving it. It can be done directly, with no apparent previous qualification. I say apparent because the effect of yoga practice is cumulative and carried over from efforts in one's past lives.

"By virtue of the divine consciousness of his previous life, he automatically becomes attracted to the yogic principles — even without seeking them. Such an inquisitive transcendentalist, striving for yoga, stands always above the ritualistic principles of the scriptures."

— Bhagavad-Gītā 6.44

Both religion and yoga mean "to link" with the divine Source. The difference is that religion is for a group; yoga is for the individual.

The key for making this crucial connection is the spiritual master.

The Philosopher's Stone

"When Parvata Muni saw the ecstatic loving symptoms of the hunter, he told Nārada, 'Certainly you are a touchstone.'"

— Caitanya-Caritāmṛta, Madhya 24.277

This quote refers to an incident mentioned in the Śrīmad-Bhāgavatam where the exalted sage Nārada Muni had converted a cruel hunter into a holy man. Formerly the hunter had taken a perverse pleasure in half-killing animals and watching them die, yet by the association of the Nārada he became peaceful and loving — to the point where he would not even harm an ant. Talk about magic!

As we are about to see, this alchemical metaphor is quite appropriate.

In alchemy there is such a thing as a touchstone, an unknown substance which turns iron into gold. The Encyclopedia Britannica states:

"Inasmuch as alchemy was concerned with the perfection of the human soul, the philosopher's stone was thought to cure illnesses, prolong life, and bring about spiritual revitalization... The philosopher's stone, variously described, was sometimes said to be a common substance, found everywhere but unrecognized and unappreciated."

In a material world of incessant competition, a genuine spiritual master (who has no desire for fame or followers) can easily go unrecognized. Now what are the qualifications of such a rare teacher?

तस्माद् गुरुं प्रपद्येत जिज्ञासुः श्रेय उत्तमम्
शाब्दे परे च निष्णातं ब्रह्मण्युपशमाश्रयम् ॥ २१॥

tasmād gurum prapadyeta
jijñāsuḥ śreya uttamam
śābde pare ca niṣṇātam
brahmaṇy upaśamāśrayam

"Any person who is seriously desirous of achieving real happiness must seek out a bona fide spiritual master and take shelter of him by initiation. The qualification of a spiritual master is that he must have realized the conclusion of the scriptures by deliberation and arguments and thus be able to convince others of these conclusions. Such great personalities, who have taken complete shelter of the Supreme Godhead, leaving aside all material considerations, are to be understood as bonafide spiritual masters." (SB 11.3.21)

Even a moment's association with a pure devotee of the Lord can begin a total spiritual transformation in another person. And there is no higher blessing. *tulayāma lavenāpi na svargam nāpunar-bhavam bhagavat-saṅgi-saṅgasya martyānām kim utāśiṣaḥ* (Śrīmad-Bhāgavatam 4.30.34) It is far better than taking birth on the material heavenly planets (the goal of the karma-yogi) or even merging into the oneness of the great spiritual light (goal of the jñāna-yogi). Both of these results are temporary.

Then there is the knock off or unlicensed copy item.

"In the *Padma Purāṇa* it is said, *sampradāya-vihīnā ye mantrās te niṣphalā matāḥ:* if one does not follow the four recognized disciplic successions, his *mantra* or initiation is useless. In the present day there are many *apasampradāyas,* or *sampradāyas* [lineages or schools] which are not bona fide, which have no link to authorities like Lord Brahmā, Lord Śiva, the Kumāras or Lakṣmī. People are misguided by such *sampradāyas.* The *śāstras* say that being initiated in such a *sampradāya* is a useless waste of time, for it will never enable one to understand the real religious principles."

— Śrīmad-Bhāgavatam 6.3.20-21, purport

Beware of imitations.

The Elixir of Immortality

The western alchemists also believed that an "elixir of life" could be derived from the Philosopher's Stone. The idea being that, the more one drinks of this nectar, his life is prolonged and he becomes immortal. That sounds like a perfect analogy for the spiritual master distributing the mahā-mantra (great chanting for deliverance).

हरे कृष्ण हरे कृष्ण
कृष्ण कृष्ण हरे हरे
हरे राम हरे राम
राम राम हरे हरे
Hare Krishna Hare Krishna
Krishna Krishna Hare Hare
Hare Rama Hare Rama
Rama Rama Hare Hare

These are names of God and His energy. The meaning is "O Supreme Lord, O Divine Energy of the Lord, kindly engage me in Your service." The prayer is not asking for advantages or benefits or daily bread; rather it is asking God, "What can I do for You?"

There are three types of chanting.

1. Mānasa - quiet chanting in mind
2. Upāmsa - silent chanting which is so soft that only the chanter himself can hear it.
3. Vacik - loud chanting which everyone can hear.

One who chants silently liberates only himself. But one who chants loudly liberates himself and any other living entity who hears him. The elixir is that powerful.

Simply put, there are many gods who manage material affairs, but Lord Viṣṇu is the Supreme Personality of Godhead, their boss. You might say that Lord Viṣṇu is Krishna when He is at the office.

One of His foremost employees, the lord of death, gives this opinion:

एतावानेव लोकेऽस्मिन् पुंसां धर्मः स्मृतः।
भक्तियोगो भगवति तन्नामग्रहणादिभिः ॥२२॥

etāvān eva loke 'smin
pumsām dharmaḥ paraḥ smṛtaḥ
bhakti-yogo bhagavati
tan-nāma-grahaṇādibhiḥ

"Devotional service, beginning with the chanting of the holy name of the Lord, is the ultimate religious principle for the living entity in human society."
— Lord Yamarāja, SB 6.3.22

The name of the Supreme Lord is non-different from Himself; chanting is association with Him. Therefore, when it comes to Bhakti-yoga, as soon as one sets foot on the path he arrives at the destination.

"Our father who art in heaven, hallowed be thy name." I used to say this prayer often in my youth, but I never knew the Supreme Lord's name until my spiritual master told me. His name is Krishna — the "all attractive." He attracts everyone and everything because He is the generating source of all energies. Krishna consciousness is our natural state of healthy life. Material consciousness is the disease. Bhakti-yoga is the cure.

What follows is a little Vedic evidence to support this premise. There is so much more.

जरयत्याशु या कोशं निगीर्णमनालो यथा ॥ ३३॥

jarayaty āśu yā kośaṁ

nigīrṇam analo yathā

"Bhakti, devotional service, dissolves the subtle body of the living entity without separate effort, just as fire in the stomach digests all that we eat."

— Lord Kapiladeva, SB 3.25.33

"For those who are engaged in the devotional service of the Supreme Personality of Godhead, all sinful reactions [*karma*], whether fructified, in the stock, or in the form of a seed, gradually vanish."

— Padma Purāṇa

"Living beings who are entangled in the complicated meshes of birth and death can be freed immediately by even unconsciously chanting the holy name of Kṛṣṇa, which is feared by fear personified."

— the sages at Naimiṣāraṇya, SB 1.1.14

THE SWORD OF REMEMBRANCE

यदनुध्यासिना युक्ताः कर्मग्रन्थिनिबन्धनं।
छिन्दन्ति कोविदास्तस्य को न कुर्यात्कथारतिम् ॥१५॥

yad-anudhyāsinā yuktāḥ
karma-granthi-nibandhanam
chindanti kovidās tasya
ko na kuryāt kathā-ratim

"With sword in hand, intelligent men cut through the binding knots of reactionary work [karma] by remembering the Personality of Godhead. Therefore, who will not pay attention to His message?" (SB 1.2.15)

It may be worth noting that Śrīmad-Bhāgavatam is not an ancient novel. Vyasadeva, the compiler of Vedic knowledge, had no market for mythological stories with no factual basis. His mission was to preserve the spiritual knowledge being handed down for future generations. These narrations of stories and conversations concerning the Lord and His pastimes are true and hearing them is drinking the nectar of immortality (rasāmṛta) through one's ears.

The Absolute Truth is not only stranger than fiction — He is way more fascinating.

"Ahaṁ brahmāsmi" means "I am spirit." Now how to act like it?

Here are instructions on how to enter the kingdom of God here on earth, given by God Himself, Lord Krishna (Bhagavad-Gītā 18.45-49).

"By following his qualities of work, every man can become perfect. Now please hear from Me how this can be done.

By worship of the Lord, who is the source of all beings and who is all-pervading, man can, in the performance of his own duty, attain perfection.

It is better to engage in one's own occupation [scholar, administrator, merchant, worker], even though one may perform it imperfectly, than to accept another's occupation and perform it perfectly. Prescribed duties, according to one's nature, are never affected by sinful reactions.

Every endeavor is covered by some sort of fault, just as fire is covered by smoke. Therefore one should not give up the work which is born of his nature, O son of Kunti, even if such work is full of fault.

One can obtain the results of renunciation simply by self-control and by becoming unattached to material things and disregarding material enjoyments. That is the highest perfectional stage of renunciation."

In other words there is no need to leave home and go to the forest to meditate alone. Stay in your occupation and do your duty. Simply change your consciousness, which He outlines next (Bhagavad-Gītā 18.50-58):

"O son of Kunti, learn from Me in brief how one can attain to the supreme perfectional stage, Brahman, by acting in the way which I shall now summarize.

Being purified by his intelligence and controlling the mind with determination, giving up the objects of sense gratification, being freed from attachment and hatred, one who lives in a secluded place, who eats little and who controls the body and the tongue, and is always in trance and is detached, who is without false ego, false strength, false pride, lust, anger, and who does not accept material things, such a person is certainly elevated to the position of self-realization.

One who is thus transcendentally situated at once realizes the Supreme Brahman. He never laments nor desires to have anything; he is equally disposed to every living entity. In that state he attains pure devotional service unto Me.

One can understand the Supreme Personality as He is only by devotional service. And when one is in full consciousness of the Supreme Lord by such devotion, he can enter into the kingdom of God.

Though engaged in all kinds of activities, My devotee,

under My protection, reaches the eternal and imperishable abode by My grace.

In all activities just depend upon Me and work always under My protection. In such devotional service, be fully conscious of Me.

If you become conscious of Me, you will pass over all the obstacles of conditional life by My grace. If, however, you do not work in such consciousness but act through false ego, not hearing Me, you will be lost."

Krishna has a knack for covering a lot of information in only a few words. In depth explanations of these points, in language that is easy to understand, can be found in the original 1972 edition of A.C. Bhaktivedanta Swami Prabhupāda's Bhagavad-gītā As It Is. Begin there.

"In some respects I am looking to a new age. But I want to do it by reinvesting ourselves in ancient tradition, not by re-inventing some homogenous, shallow, easy-to-swallow misrepresentation of those traditions."

— David Life, Jivamukti Yoga

There are as many theories for understanding the ultimate truth of life as there are philosophers. Indeed, the qualification for being a philosopher is that one must come up with a new theory. The New Age Movement encompassed an eclectic mix of Western esoteric studies from the eighteenth through twentieth centuries, with roots going back to far earlier times. These included spiritism, channeling, Theosophy, Jungian depth psychology, holistic alternative medicine and Ayurveda, hatha-yoga, pagan rituals and so on. Despite their claims, however, these paths do not all lead to the same destination.

In an effort to understand life and reality, there are two processes for acquiring knowledge: the ascending method and the descending method. The first relies upon rational thinking to arrive at conclusions. If one is honest he will admit this method is imperfect. This is due to the illusory effect that material energy has upon consciousness.

"As the different limbs of the body cannot see the eyes, the living entities cannot see the Supreme Lord, who is situated as the Supersoul in everyone's heart. Not by the senses, by the mind, by the life air, by thoughts within the heart, or by the vibration of words can the living entities ascertain the real situation of the Supreme Lord.

— Yamarāja, lord of death, SB 6.3.16

The descending method is recommended since the knowledge is perfect, handed down from the perfect source.

"Just try to learn the truth by approaching a spiritual master. Inquire from him submissively and render service unto him. The self-realized soul can impart knowledge unto you because he has seen the truth.

And when you have thus learned the truth, you will know that all living beings are but part of Me — and that they are in Me, and are Mine."

— Bhagavad-Gītā 4.34-35

Spiritual alchemy is Bhakti yoga, the process of purification of the soul (anartha-nivṛtti). It begins with hearing about, chanting and remembering Krishna, the Supreme Personality of Godhead, the Absolute Truth. Here are the books to study:

1. Bhagavad-Gītā As It Is
2. Śrīmad-Bhāgavatam (Bhāgavat Purāṇa)

3. Nectar of Devotion (Bhakti-rasāmṛta-sindhu)
4. Teachings of Lord Caitanya (Śrī Caitanya-caritāmṛta)

The word amṛta (see titles 3 and 4 above) means nectar, the elixir of life — of immortality, knowledge and happiness, sac-cid-ānanda. Study of these literatures is drinking the nectar that nourishes the soul, and it is recommended by authorities (mahātmās).

"O expert and thoughtful men, relish Śrīmad-Bhāgavatam, the mature fruit of the desire tree of Vedic literatures. It emanated from the lips of Śrī Śukadeva Gosvāmī. Therefore this fruit has become even more tasteful, although its nectarean juice was already relishable for all, including liberated souls."

— Śrīmad-Bhāgavatam 1.1.3

True healing means taking one's attachment to material things and transmuting it into attachment for Krishna or God. This is the spiritual alchemy of turning iron into gold — developing loving attachment to the Supreme Lord and reviving one's eternal relationship with Him.

He's been waiting for you forever and He is not going to let you go.

The question is: Are you ready now?

ADDENDUM

The Perennial Philosophy Returns

"The perennial philosophy suggests that when you consider all the spiritual traditions throughout the ages which have been articulated in different languages, there is a core tendency, a common truth that is evident. It has never died, it has always been kept alive in some way or another …The emerging worldview is the perennial philosophy modified to take into account recent historical and scientific developments."

— Mark Woodhouse, PhD., Georgia State University

Features:

1. There is a dimensional interpenetration.
2. Levels of reality differ by degree of density.
3. Seeing the spiritual oneness (brahman) in all things.
4. God (Parabrahman) is not just the sum total of all things.
5. Reincarnation.
6. Takes paranormal abilities seriously.
7. Sees "spiritual growth" as the reason why we're here.
8. Does NOT say all religions provide different

paths to the same truth, or that they are pretty much the same.

A FINAL WORD

Occult means hidden. There is a reason why there were secret societies who studied these hidden truths of life. Remember Galileo and the Inquisition: If the world you see is different from what others see, keep your magic secret. Unpopular truths are heresy.

Born in Saint Louis, Missouri, throughout her life Sravaniya has been interested in metaphysics, spirituality and comparative religion. She became a vegetarian at the age of seventeen and began studying eastern classics to understand consciousness and reality. "I've always been interested in subjects that had no commercial potential," she says. "I guess I'm your friendly neighborhood occult specialist." Times have certainly changed and more people are interested in these subjects. Using her decades of experience, Sravaniya provides a link to the most reliable sources. Her writings connect the underlying truths of Western philosophy with the reliable scriptural evidence of the East. Informative, thought provoking and entertaining.

She took formal initiation from A.C. Bhaktivedanta Swami Prabhupada (Brahma-Gaudiya Vaisnava sampradaya) in 1971, spent decades studying classical Sanskrit texts in yoga ashrams around the world. She was instrumental in getting Srila Prabhupada's Bhagavad-Gita As It Is translated into Chinese. In 2006 she published a study guide for the English version of her guru's seminal work entitled Basic Bhagavad Gita: An Introduction to Bhagavat Vedanta. Now the revised 2017 second edition is available in eBook format.

She also taught hatha yoga in the Far East since 1983 and in the early 90s was the first professional yoga teacher in Hong Kong. She has studied yoga with many senior teachers from the Iyengar and K. Pattabhi Jois traditions. She received yoga certification in the Sivananda lineage from Swami Visnudevananda himself some 22 years after learning her first asanas from his book.

A Yoga Alliance E-RYT 500 instructor, she conducted yoga teachers training and certifications in Hong Kong between 2004-06. Currently she is teaching guided study certificate courses in Bhagavad Gita.

Sravaniya has also been an astrological and psychic consultant since 1992 and her clients include people from all walks of life and diverse cultures. She has been featured in a variety of publications including The Asian Wall Street Journal, the South China Morning Post, Hong Kong Standard, HK Magazine and others, and has appeared on CNBC as well as local television and radio.

Sravaniya has two sons who are pursuing yoga and

martial arts. She lives in Hong Kong with her husband, Dhananjay Kulkarni.

For more information:
www.BarefootPhilosopher.Press
info@BarefootPhilosopher.Press

www.ingramcontent.com/pod-product-compliance
Lightning Source LLC
Chambersburg PA
CBHW031347160726
47993CB00002B/861